The New Star

by Taffy Davies

Space illustrations by Mike Carroll
Biblical Illustrations by Victor Ambrus

A TAMARIND BOOK

When you look at the night sky you can see thousands of stars. It's impossible to see them all from earth. They are so far away that they appear to form patterns or constellations in the sky. Some of the constellations have been given names, like The Bear and Orion the Hunter. They are constantly changing, slowly moving and developing. Some stars are very new and have only recently been born; others are growing cold and dark and eventually fade and die. When some stars die they explode into the brightest of lights and go out with a "bang". These are called supernova.

About 2000 years ago a bright star shone in the sky over a country called Palestine and a city called Bethlehem. It coincided with the birth of a baby called Jesus.

When the star appeared in the sky it was noticed and recorded by some Magi, wise men or astrologers, who then left their own eastern country, convinced that the star meant that a new king had been born.

No one knows for certain what the new star, the Bethlehem star, was. It had been foretold in ancient Jewish writings that a new star would appear at the birth of Jesus. It could have been a comet, like Halley's comet, or it could have been two planets meeting or coming very close together. It could have been a supernova, a rare and special event, to mark the arrival of the baby king into the world.

Whatever happened and however it came about, a new star did appear in the sky. It was the way God planned it, just as God planned to send Jesus into the world at a particular place and time.

In the beginning there was nothing.

There was nothing above the nothing, and there was nothing under the nothing. The nothing had nothing at the start, and the nothing had nothing at the end. It was a nothing with no tomorrow and it was a nothing with no yesterday.

Then out of the nothing came the voice of God.

"Let there be light!" God said, and immediately the nothing splintered and shattered.

Out of the big black nothing of space, God made light and darkness, day and night. Out of the nothing God made the stars and the galaxies, the heavens and the earth. In the midst of this hissing cauldron of creation, God breathed on the tiny, spinning planet called earth, and here life began.

God filled the universe with galaxies that spiralled and spun. He formed burning gases into stars and from these stars he formed planets, and set them in their places. God swirled patterns with dusty gases on the inky blackness of space as billions of stars and comets hissed and hurled themselves at one another.

God chose one particular star, as it tumbled through space, and positioned it ready to burst into life at a particular time in history, one chosen moment, to coincide with a special and amazing event.

High above the earth, there were billions of stars studding the universe. Only a few of them, the very brightest or the very nearest, could be seen by the people who lived on earth.

One star, the chosen star, shone out and sparkled like many others as comets rumbled past it in the darkness of space. It was not the brightest star in the universe but it had not yet fully developed. Its time had not yet come.

The chosen star continued to shine. It witnessed the birth of bright new stars. It saw them collapse in on themselves and die, creating black holes in the universe. The star continued to wait for the moment God had made it for, the special moment when it would burst into the brightest of lights and be visible to the people living on the earth.

In the deep darkness of space, the chosen star sparkled and shone. If people on earth had looked long and hard they might have spotted tiny specks of stars beyond the very brightest in the dark night sky. But the chosen star was still invisible, still too faint to be seen above the billions of others, still waiting for its special moment.

The planet earth, with its areas of green and blue, land and giant oceans, continued to spin in space, and circle round its own star, the sun.

Around the earth there was a thin band of atmosphere, set like a protective shield around the tiny planet. The earth spun and circled around its sun, half in light, half in darkness; not too near to be too hot, or too far away to be too cold.

The planet earth did not have Saturn's rings or Neptune's deep blue atmosphere, but God loved it and had a special purpose for the people who lived on it.

The chosen star, still silent in space, also had a purpose, and the time was drawing near for the world to know how it fitted into the great plan.

Everything was now in place.

The chosen star still shone, unnoticed, unseen, in the heavens. The time had come for God to enter the world he had made by becoming a human being himself. It was the rescue plan God had set in operation at the beginning of time.

The chosen star started to change.

Its already burning hot temperature rose yet higher and higher. Its already enormous pressure became yet greater and greater, forcing it into an enormous and glorious explosion of shining light. Now the time for the chosen star to burn brightly in the heavens had come. It shone out more brightly than any other star in the galaxy. It sparkled more brightly than the sun from which the earth took its light.

The chosen star sparkled and shone between the other stars, burning still more brightly, allowing its radiant light to point the way to the weary travellers.

The star outshone and outsparkled everything else in the heavens. It had fulfilled its purpose. God had created it for this moment.

The chosen star was the brightest light in the sky, brighter than a comet and longer lasting than a coming together of the planets. It was like an arrow from heaven to guide the travellers to the baby Jesus. It was brighter than the light of the sun and it poured its light upon the earth, and upon the child who would be a light to the world.

The chosen star still sparkled in the night sky, high above the earth. It no longer guided human travellers, but shone still brighter and hotter than the sun. Yet deep within its core the star began to fade and cool. The radiant beams which had reached the earth had become fainter, less bright now, more like the other stars. Although it was steadily burning, it was also cooling.

The star had been in existence since the creation of the universe and God had set it in the heavens for a specific purpose. Now it had completed its task.

The star was beginning to die.

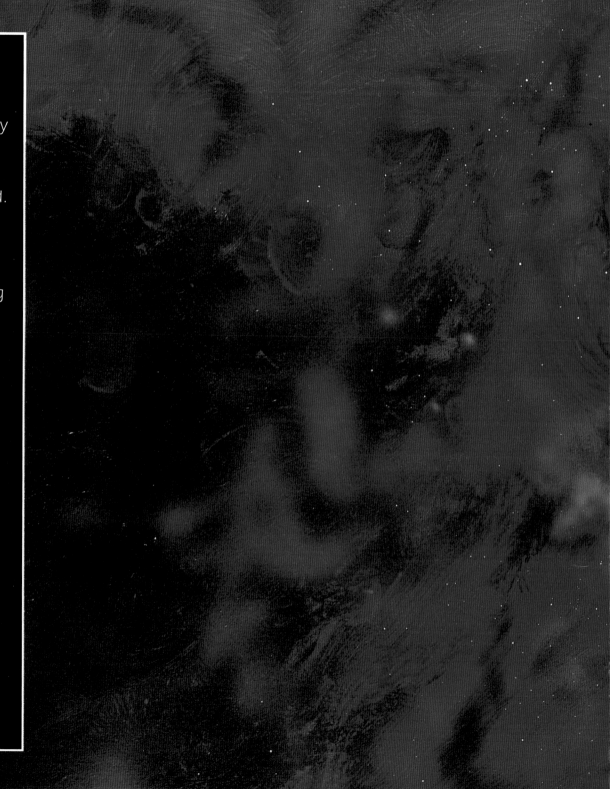

The special star grew colder. Its fiery heat still smouldered, but the daytime sky had turned black. None of the stars were shining now. The light had gone out of the world.

It was then that the star's core began to collapse in on itself. It disappeared and caved in, heaving and throwing off its gases deep into space. Then with one massive movement it exploded inwards.

Then there was nothing but a black hole. The star had died.

A Tamarind Book
Published in association with SU Publishing
207-209 Queensway, Bletchley, Milton Keynes, Bucks
ISBN 1 873824 77 7

First edition 1997

Text endorsed by Ian Morison,
Nuffield Radio Astronomy Laboratories, Jodrell Bank

Printed and bound in Singapore